Explore Space!

Walking on the Moon

by Deborah A. Shearer

Consultant:
James Gerard
Aerospace Education Specialist
NASA Aerospace Education Services Program

Bridgestone Books
an imprint of Capstone Press
Mankato, Minnesota

Bridgestone Books are published by Capstone Press
151 Good Counsel Drive, P.O. Box 669, Mankato, Minnesota 56002
http://www.capstone-press.com

Library of Congress Cataloging-in-Publication Data
Shearer, Deborah A.
    Walking on the moon / by Deborah A. Shearer.
    p. cm.—(Explore space!)
    Includes bibliographical references and index.
    Summary: Describes what it was like for astronauts to walk on the Moon during the
Apollo missions.
    ISBN 0-7368-1145-1
    1. Extravehicular activity (Manned space flight)—Juvenile literature. 2. Moon—
Exploration—Juvenile literature. 3. Moon—Surface—Juvenile literature. 4. Project Apollo
(U.S.)—Juvenile literature. [1. Moon—Exploration. 2. Project Apollo (U.S.) 3. Astronautics.]
I. Title. II. Series.
TL1096 .S53 2002
919.9'104—dc21   2001003590

Editorial Credits
Tom Adamson, editor; Karen Risch, product planning editor; Steve Christensen,
    cover designer; Linda Clavel, production designer and illustrator; Katy Kudela,
    photo researcher

Photo Credits
© Digital Vision, cover, 4, 14, 22
NASA, 6, 10, 12, 16, 18, 20
NASA/TOM STACK & ASSOCIATES, 8

1 2 3 4 5 6 07 06 05 04 03 02

Table of Contents

Edwin "Buzz" Aldrin

The First Moonwalk

On July 20, 1969, Neil Armstrong and Buzz Aldrin became the first people to walk on the Moon. Ten more astronauts walked on the Moon during the next three years. These flights to the Moon were called the Apollo missions.

astronaut
a person who is trained to live and work in space

Why Did Astronauts Go to the Moon?

Scientists wanted to know what the Moon is like. They wanted to know if astronauts could travel safely to the Moon. Astronauts brought back 843 pounds (382 kilograms) of Moon rock and soil for scientists to study.

The Moon's Gravity

The Moon's gravity is one-sixth of Earth's gravity. Objects on the Moon weigh less than they weigh on Earth. The Moon's gravity allowed astronauts to jump higher on the Moon than on Earth. They had to move less weight.

gravity
the force that pulls objects down toward the surface of Earth and the Moon

What Is It Like to Walk on the Moon?

The Moon's soil is powdery. It stuck to astronauts' space suits and boots. Astronauts could hop around like kangaroos. They could not stop easily because their space suits were stiff.

Lunar rovers could travel about 8 miles (13 kilometers) per hour. That speed is about twice as fast as a person normally walks.

Lunar Rovers

Walking on the Moon for many hours was tiring. Astronauts used lunar rovers during the last three Apollo missions. These electric cars allowed astronauts to travel farther away from their base. They wore seat belts to keep from bouncing up and floating off the rover.

The Moon's Surface

The Moon does not have oceans, lakes, or rivers. There are no plants or animals. The surface is covered with rocks and craters. The Moon's soil is gray and dusty. Every step the astronauts made left a footprint.

crater
a hole in the ground made by a meteorite

A pole was placed in the top of the flag planted by astronauts. There is no wind on the Moon to blow the flag. The pole keeps the flag from drooping.

Atmosphere

The Moon has no atmosphere. There is no oxygen to breathe. Astronauts wore space suits on moonwalks so they could breathe. With no atmosphere, the sky is black and very clear. Astronauts' helmets had sun visors to protect their eyes from the bright sunlight.

atmosphere
the mixture of gases that surrounds some planets and moons

17

"It's a stark and strangely different place, but it looked friendly to me and it proved to be friendly." —Neil Armstrong

crater

Is There Life on the Moon?

Astronauts did not find any signs of life on the Moon. Rocks that were brought back do not contain any fossils. Studies done by scientists proved that water never flowed on the Moon.

fossil
the preserved remains of a plant or animal

This NASA painting shows what future exploration might look like on the Moon.

Future Life on the Moon

People hope to return to the Moon someday. Geologists want to study the rocks and soil. Astronomers want to bring telescopes to the Moon. Doctors hope to study how people adapt to living on the Moon.

telescope
an instrument that makes objects appear larger and closer

Hands On: Make a Moon Footprint

Every footprint that has been made on the Moon is still there. There is no water or wind to wear them away.

What You Need

Flat, rectangular cake pan
Several cups of flour
Glue stick
Black construction paper
Old sneaker or tennis shoe
Damp cloth

What You Do

1. Fill the cake pan about 1 inch (2.5 centimeters) deep with flour.
2. Spread glue from the glue stick on a piece of black construction paper.
3. Put on an old tennis shoe. Wipe the bottom of the shoe with a damp cloth.
4. Step carefully into the flour.
5. Step lightly on the construction paper. This will make a footprint that you can keep.
6. Also notice the footprint lines in the pan. This was what the astronauts saw with each step and what still can be seen on the Moon.

Words to Know

astronomer (uh-STRON-uh-mur)—a person who studies stars, planets, and outer space

atmosphere (AT-muhss-feehr)—the mixture of gases that surrounds some planets and moons; the Moon has no atmosphere.

exploration (ek-spluh-RAY-shuhn)—the study of an unknown place

gravity (GRAV-uh-tee)—a force that pulls objects together; gravity pulls objects down toward the surface of Earth and the Moon.

oxygen (OK-suh-juhn)—a colorless gas that people need to breathe

visor (VYE-zur)—a shield on the front of a helmet; a visor protected astronauts' eyes from the Sun's bright glare.

Read More

Goldsmith, Mike. *Neil Armstrong: The First Man in the Moon.* Famous Lives. Austin, Texas: Raintree Steck-Vaughn, 2001.

Kelly, Nigel. *The Moon Landing: The Race into Space.* Point of Impact. Chicago: Heinemann, 2001.

Stott, Carole. *Moon Landing: The Race for the Moon.* DK Discoveries. New York: DK, 1999.

Internet Sites

NASA Kids—Space & Beyond
http://kids.msfc.nasa.gov/Space
The Nine Planets—The Moon
http://www.staq.qld.edu.au/k9p/moon.htm

Index